SOARING OVER THE VALLEY

SOARING OVER THE VALLEY

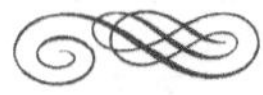

Follow me on my health challenge with 40 days of God-inspired Devotions

KATHLEEN J. GOODEN

Soaring Daily Devotions

First Printing, 2024

Unless otherwise noted, all Scripture quotations are taken from the English Standard Version® (ESV®). © 2001 by Crossway, a publishing ministry of Good News Publishers. ESV Text Edition: 2016. Used by permission. All rights reserved.

Scripture quotations marked NIV are from The Holy Bible, New International Version® (NIV®). Copyright © 1973, 1978, 1984, 2011 by Biblica, Inc.® Used by permission. All rights reserved worldwide.

Scripture quotations marked NLT are from the Holy bible, New Living Translation © 1996, 2004, 2007, 2013, 2015 by Tyndale House Foundation. Used by permission by Tyndale House Publishers, Inc., Carol Stream, Illinois 60188. All rights reserved.

Cover design: Andrea Moxam

ISBN: 9798218420376 (Paperback)
ISBN: 9798218420611 (eBook)

Contents

Introduction

As they go through the Valley of Baca they make it a place of springs; the early rain also covers it with pools.—Psalm 84:6

In his book *Secrets of the Secret Place*, Bob Sorge explains that we are to confess our confidence in the One who is enabling us to turn the darkness of our valley "into a place of springs and pools—into a fruitful garden."

Such has been my experience for the past year when a cancer diagnosis hit me in the face—almost literally. Cancer was found on the inside of my mouth and, as a result, affected my face, my smile, my look, and my outlook. Like many people receiving such a diagnosis, I wept (Baca in the text above means *weeping*), among other emotions that will be described in this devotional. But through it all, I grew from weakness to strength, despair to victory, and darkness into light as I saw this diagnosis change my trust and confidence in God.

Whether you are a believer in Jesus Christ or someone who discovered this devotional by chance, the journey you are about to embark on will give you the confidence needed to mount up and soar over any adversity in your life—present or future. It is my hope that you will increase your faith, strength, courage, and endurance while soaring over and watching your valley become a fruitful garden.

BACKGROUND

I began my unexpected cancer journey when I was diagnosed with parotid gland cancer, an extremely rare and aggressive form of cancer. There was a large malignant tumor located on my right parotid gland, which required the complete removal of this gland along with the facial nerve on the right side of my face. The doctors used a surgical procedure known as a radical parotidectomy. The tumor removal required extensive reconstructive surgery and radiation therapy. While on this journey, I experienced a roller coaster of emotional and physical pain and what seemed like a fierce battle that would never end. It was from this place of weeping that I gained a greater understanding of God's peace and a deeper dependence on His strength, and I am almost certain that this understanding would not have occurred had I not had this dreadful illness. And with each twist and turn, detour, confusing turn, sudden stop, and every rough patch along the path of this journey, I have learned to trust in God's ability, allowed His will to determine the outcome in my situation, and have grown in perseverance through reliance on God, who is my "Wonderful Counselor, Mighty God, Everlasting Father, Prince of Peace" (Isaiah 9:6). And with the spiritual strengthening (or comfort) and encouragement that I received through daily prayer and meditation on His written Word, God has prepared me to spiritually strengthen and encourage others in the future who may have a similar journey (2 Corinthians 4:1).

My love for journaling substantially contributed to my ability to remember the many details of my experience. This helped me to retain God's spiritual truths and provided the strength I needed to progress on this journey.

HOW TO USE THIS BOOK

In this devotional book, you will find many encouraging scriptures, short stories about my health journey, thought-provoking questions, and simple prayers to help you focus your heart and mind on what it takes to soar over the valley. Take time to read and ponder each day's material, and reflect on the questions while allowing God to speak to you through His words. During the next forty days, you will gain insight into my journey and discover ways to increase your faith, strength, courage, and endurance while soaring over any adversity you may face.

One

April Fools' Day

Shortly after releasing my first book in March 2023, I was diagnosed with an extremely rare and aggressive type of cancer known as parotid gland cancer. This type of cancer makes up less than one percent of all cancers diagnosed in the US every year. Most people have never even heard of the parotid gland, let alone this type of cancer diagnosis. The Mayo Clinic's website provides us with this insight: "Parotid tumors are growths of cells that start in the parotid glands. The parotid glands are two salivary glands that sit just in front of the ears. There is one on each side of the face. Salivary glands make saliva to help with chewing and digesting food. There are many salivary glands in the lips, cheeks, mouth, and throat. Growths of cells, which are called tumors, can happen in any of these glands. The parotid glands are the most common place that salivary gland tumors happen."

My main symptom was constant and often excruciating jaw pain. After almost eight months of seeing one medical professional after another, I finally saw an ENT doctor (otolaryngologist) who ordered a biopsy of the suspicious area located in and around the parotid gland. I waited days for the biopsy results, torn between what those results could mean and being relieved that I was getting closer to having a diagnosis. When I finally received the agonizing news of the presence of cancer in the parotid gland, the world stood still. It so happened that my doctor delivered this news to me on Saturday, April 1, 2023. It was almost as if it were an April Fools' joke—the first day of April having been associated with comedy for centuries. I remember that day very well. I was speechless, shocked, angry, anxious, and sad. A fierce avalanche of emotions gripped me.

My cancer diagnosis was neither a joke nor a prank. And this was no random day. God chose this day to bring me this grim news to help me to always remember this one thing: He already knows about all the events that will happen in my life. David, the psalmist, says in his song and praise to God that God knows the days that were formed for me (Psalm 139:16), indicating that He knew our steps and planned them, and He is in control. He also knows how our steps will be ordered (Job 31:4), and even the hairs of our head are all numbered (Luke 12:7). Not many things in our lives happen by fate, chance, luck, or coincidence.

Reflect: How do you see God's hand at work in your daily life?

Prayer: Lord, I praise You because You are in control of all things. Thank You for knowing all the events that will happen in my life. Please help me to trust Your daily plan. In Jesus's name, amen.

Two

God's Faithfulness

> *Because you know that the testing of your faith produces persever-*
> *ance.*
> *James 1:3, NIV*

A few days after my cancer diagnosis, my mind jumped into overdrive. My first thought was severe sickness, followed by what seemed like a death sentence. I felt emotions like sadness, anxiety, loneliness, fear, and grief. I told myself, "You are never going to be the same." I asked questions like how did I get this? What caused this? What is the survival rate? How far along is the cancer? Is it terminal? Will my loved ones be able to cope with this news? What are the treatment options? Every day, I googled anything I could find about parotid or salivary gland cancer. The more information, images, and videos I found on the Internet, the deeper I began slipping down the rabbit hole—and I did not know how to climb back out of it.

Years ago, I asked some of those same questions when I had

an ectopic pregnancy, which almost took away my chance of ever having any children. Later in my life, I started having frequent panic attacks and severe anxiety that were debilitating. Now I found myself battling cancer—the dreaded *C* word—to mimic an expression well known in our culture. These were some of the traumatic events in my life that tested my faith in God and reshaped who I am today. We will all encounter the testing of our faith at some point, and it may feel like God is not there when we are going through our struggles, when we feel like we have no more fight left in us. However, I once learned that the teacher is often silent during the test. The Bible story of Job has a lot to say about the depth of despair that we can sink into when certain trials overtake us. I can remember seeking encouragement from Job during those long days and fearful nights. Job understood God's testing when he said, "But he knows the way that I take; when he has tried me, I shall come out as gold" (Job 23:10). God allows and has specific purposes for the "testing of your faith," just as the verse from James at the beginning of this chapter shares. James tells us that it produces perseverance (James 1:2–4, Romans 5:3) and develops character that is pleasing to God, which effectively makes us spiritually mature and stronger.

As our faith is being tested, we must remember that God is faithful to meet our needs in so many ways. God's faithfulness yesterday is a promise of His faithfulness tomorrow. In His faithfulness to me, He gifted me with three beautiful children and showed me how to manage my anxiety and panic attacks. He will be just as faithful on my cancer journey. His faithfulness will never run out (2 Timothy 2:13).

Reflect: How has your faith been tested? How are you responding to your tests?

Prayer: Dear God, thank You for always being with me during my trials. Help me to remember Your past faithfulness, that I will become strong in my faith, and to fully trust You. In Jesus's name, amen.

Three

Miracles

For days, I patiently waited for a phone call from the doctor that would tell me there was some kind of mistake. I was expecting him to say that I do not have cancer. I was desperately looking for a big miracle. The Bible is full of miracles. Among them, God parted the Red Sea, sent food down from the sky, and raised Jesus from the dead. Jesus also performed many other miracles, including turning water into wine, healing the lame and blind, and bringing dead people back to life. In fact, when the angel spoke to Jesus's mother, Mary, before the birth of her son, he said to her, "For with God, nothing will be impossible" (Luke 1:37). God works miracles and wonders (Psalm 77:14), and He is the source of all miracles.

But I never received any such phone call from the doctor. The big miracle I was praying for did not happen. The testing of my faith continued. Somehow, I was very grateful for every tiny glimmer of a miracle that God provided in my life during this time, such as the referral I received from a friend for an ENT surgeon. This surgeon was a surgical expert in treating cancerous tumors of the head and neck. I was filled with expectancy upon learning about his impeccable skills that I could lean on in my time of need. Another miracle was the speed with which I was scheduled for surgery after my consultation. It normally takes weeks, if not months, of waiting, but miraculously, there was an opening in four weeks. God was teaching me how to become more attentive to the small miracles happening right there before my eyes and within my grasp. The challenge is slowing down long enough and often enough to become more observant and grateful for the small miracles, to be still and know that He is God (Psalm 46:10).

Reflect: Can you think of a time when God performed a miracle in your life, small or big?

Prayer: Lord, You are the same yesterday, today, and forever. Thank You for performing miracles. Help me to be more observant of the big and small miracles in my life. In Jesus's name, amen.

Four

Holding It Together

After the cancer diagnosis, I met with the ENT oncology surgeon I mentioned in the previous devotional. He practiced at one of the hospitals in my hometown and was familiar with parotid gland cancer. I found him to be a caring, confident, and knowledgeable surgeon. He explained that there was a large mass extending from my right ear down to my jaw. He ordered several imaging tests, such as an MRI and Positron Emission Tomography (PET). The PET scan was the most critical since it would show if the cancer had spread to other parts of my body. Eventually, the PET scan could also help physicians design the most beneficial cancer treatment for me.

Twenty-four hours before the PET scan test, I had strict orders to avoid all forms of nicotine, caffeine (decaf included), sugars (refined or added sugars, such as desserts or sweets), sugar substitutes, and any vigorous exercises. I did exactly as I was told. When I went for the exam the next morning, my blood glucose level was extremely low from not eating enough carbohydrates the day before. My head was hurting, and I felt extremely weak and dizzy. By the grace of God, I made it through the almost two-hour test.

I waited anxiously for several days to get the PET scan results. The results revealed that cancer was found in the right parotid gland and lymph nodes in the neck area, but it had not metastasized to my bones or organs in my body. I was so thankful for these results. Things could have been so much worse. In moments like these, we have absolute assurance and comfort in the knowledge that God is in control and knows exactly what must happen at exactly the right times in our lives: He is before all things, and in Him all things hold together (Colossians 1:17). While we do not completely understand why God allows cancer in anyone's life, we can rest in knowing that nothing we are going through is beyond the reach of His love and care.

God takes control when we wholeheartedly give ourselves to Him and allow Him to lead the way. He is holding all things together. That is a comforting thought.

Reflect: What are you trying to control? What part of your life do you need to surrender?

Prayer: God, You are all-powerful. Thank You that You hold everything together, from the stars in the heavens to the cells in my body. Help me to remember that You will hold all things together when life feels out of control. In Jesus's name, amen.

Five

Guidance

For you are my rock and my fortress; and for your name's sake you lead me and guide me.

Psalm 31:3

After all the imaging results were available, my husband and I met with the ENT oncology surgeon, who told us about what the road ahead looked like. Major surgery would be necessary to completely remove the right parotid gland and facial nerve, and this would involve a surgical procedure known as a radical right parotidectomy. It would be followed by a neck dissection to remove the lymph nodes in the neck area that might possibly contain cancer cells. Removing the parotid gland would leave a huge dent on the right side of my face, and with the removal of the right side facial nerve, I would lose the ability to fully close my right eyelid. Additionally, he explained that plastic surgery would be needed to reconstruct the right side of my face to fill the void after the removal of the affected parotid gland. I tried to stave off the shock and horror that was gripping me deep down as he explained all this. This work required the surgeon to quickly assemble his team of experts, which included a facial plastic surgeon, an ear surgeon, an anesthesiologist, and a host of other medical staff. This team's skill and expertise would be vital to successfully executing this very complex and extensive surgery.

I was extremely exhausted and stressed out. What more could I do? Amid my cancer journey, I began to intentionally count those little miracles I mentioned earlier. I realized that God had guided me to the right team of dedicated medical professionals in the right place at the right time. I found comfort in believing that God would guide the hands of the entire medical team He chose for me by giving them the skill, knowledge, and wisdom to do exactly what they needed to do. Just like I trust the navigation system in my car or on my phone to get me to my destination, God was going to give me all the guidance I needed on this cancer journey. He promises to guide me (Psalm 31:3) so that I can take the right steps at the right time. My role is to obey His directions by faith, even if it does not make sense to my natural way of thinking.

God guides us each moment of every day so that we will not need to worry about the next step. We can be sure that He will not lead us to, or leave us in, an unknown location as we might experience with a navigation system. Furthermore, the Bible tells us that His eyes are on us, and He will "instruct you and teach you in the way you should go" (Psalm 32:8).

Reflect: Who or what is guiding you through life on this earth?

Prayer: Dear God, You are good and gracious. Help me to listen to Your directions and to always trust Your directions for my life. In Jesus's name, amen.

Six

Do the Right Thing

When I shared the grim news of my cancer diagnosis with all my friends and loved ones, they were all in terrible shock. Most were in disbelief. "But you are so healthy" and "you are one of the healthiest people I know" were some of the reactions. They were right to believe this about me. Most of my life, I maintained a healthy weight, exercised daily, and made wise food and lifestyle choices like not smoking, using illicit drugs, or drinking too much alcohol. Health experts tell us that we can help fend off cancer by eating specific foods such as beans, berries, broccoli, dark leafy green vegetables, nuts, turmeric, and garlic. I ate all these foods and ended up with cancer. As a nutritionist with a nutrition consulting business, I found it extremely hard to continue teaching others how to achieve healthy eating for life. I was having a hard time believing in this message I shared with my clients for years. But discouraging thoughts have a way of eating away at what we thought were core beliefs. Thankfully, the Holy Spirit within me was telling me that this was not the right way to think (Philippians 4:8).

As a Christian, it is not always easy to do the right thing and live in obedience to God's commands given in the Bible. This is important because the Bible is our instruction manual that helps us get answers to questions like "Am I doing what it says to do?" So many times, we want to do things our own way and in our own strength, but God is our helper in times of need (Psalm 46:1). Galatians 6:9 says this: "And let us not grow weary of doing good, for in due season we will reap, if we do not give up." When we obey what God tells us to do and follow the lead of the Holy Spirit, we will get our reward at the proper time, or due season, but only if we keep on doing what is right. Not only will God reward us, but He will also give us many blessings when we obey Him (Deuteronomy 28:2, NIV).

Reflect: Are you tempted to give up when things get hard or not do the right thing?

Prayer: Lord, help me not to get weary of doing the right thing. In Jesus's name, amen.

Seven

Greater Things to Come

For I consider that the sufferings of this present time are not worth comparing with the glory that is to be revealed to us.

Romans 8:18

In the months leading up to my cancer diagnosis, I was having pain in my right jaw area, and I was noticing that the right side of my face was beginning to look a little different, like it was sagging. My husband thought it might be related to a stroke, and wanting to be cautious, we decided to go to urgent care. The urgent care doctor did not find any evidence of a stroke but instead diagnosed me with right-sided Bell's palsy (facial muscle weakness or paralysis) of unknown cause. He explained that the facial nerve on the right side of my face was completely damaged. This nerve controls the movements of muscles in the face, including the ability to smile and raise the eyebrows. I could not lift my right eyebrow, and I had a one-sided smile. My right eyelid drooped, and I had trouble pronouncing some words correctly. I made a follow-up appointment to see my primary care doctor to confirm the Bell's palsy diagnosis. She told me that symptoms should improve within a couple of months, with complete recovery within six months. After several weeks, I came to the realization that my facial paralysis was not improving. Without a doubt, I was suffering physically and mentally. Sickness has a way of consuming our every thought.

Suffering knows no strangers, and it is part of human existence. It does not matter if you are a believer or an unbeliever. People suffer from sickness, abuse, loss, depression, injury, and even seeing other people suffer. Some people seek drugs and alcohol to deal with suffering while some will go as far as seeking death to deal with their pain and sense of hopelessness. There are numerous accounts of suffering throughout the Bible. When Jesus walked the earth, He Himself endured physical torment, emotional trauma, and spiritual agony. He knows all about pain and suffering and what we are going through. In a commentary on the story of Lazarus (John 11), Joanna Weaver writes in her book *Having a Mary Heart in a Martha World* that "He [Jesus] doesn't ask anything of us that he wasn't willing to do himself and promises to be with us in all we have to go through."

Although my suffering was nothing compared to that of Jesus, the pain I experienced was unbearable at times. I often thought that this pain would never end and that things were only going to get worse. But I was reminded that our suffering will be temporary and what we will go through does not compare to the glory that is to come (Romans 8:18). We can be assured that God knows and understands our pain and is "greater than our heart, and he knows everything" (1 John 3:20). Lean heavily upon His promises and allow Him to strengthen you daily during these times of suffering, knowing that there are greater things to come.

Reflect: How have you handled suffering in your life?

Prayer: God, You are all-knowing. Thank You for being in the midst of my suffering. May Your presence strengthen me and give me courage during my suffering. In Jesus's name, amen.

Eight

God's Plans

The surgery date was set for May 16, 2023. My sister-in-law had planned a trip to Paris for the end of May, and my husband and I had been invited. The trip was planned six months in advance in celebration of her seventieth birthday. However, once the surgery date was determined, we had to cancel our travel plans because surgery could not be delayed. My husband and I were disappointed that we would not be able to join in the celebration, but we knew that there was a high risk of the cancer spreading to other parts of my body if we postponed the surgery for a later date. Furthermore, the jaw pain and facial paralysis had become so physically and emotionally draining that I would not have been able to enjoy any of the events that were planned in Paris. Having cancer was not part of my plan, but I came to accept it as part of God's plan for me, even if the timing was not right.

We all make plans, such as deciding what college to attend, what career to pursue, who to marry, where to go on vacation, and so much more. But God often has His own plans that are achieved instead of ours. A good example of God overriding human plans is in the story of Joseph. Joseph's brothers devised a plan to sell their brother into slavery (Genesis 37:1–50). However, God turned Joseph's story into a blessing, showing God's triumph over human plans.

It is good to make plans, but we must seek God's guidance and His will before executing them so that they can be carried out successfully. As we follow God's plans, we must be willing to change our plans to fit His and be willing to heed what He says —"My thoughts are nothing like your thoughts, says the Lord. And my ways are far beyond anything you could imagine" (Isaiah 55:8 NLT).

Reflect: How are you seeking God's guidance in your plans? Do you see God's guidance in your plans?

Prayer: Lord, thank You for Your guidance. Help me to remember that Your plans are always good and to always choose Your plan, not mine. I ask for Your guidance so that Your plans for me can be carried out successfully. In Jesus's name, amen.

Nine

Unlimited Strength

Two weeks before cancer surgery, I told myself that I was not going to let this diagnosis stop me from enjoying my life. I was either going to face cancer in my own strength or with the strength God provides. I chose the latter. I was devastated but not destroyed. So I decided I was not going to become a victim of my diagnosis or of any prognosis still to come. These were the options that I chose for my mental and spiritual well-being. The imminent surgery would have to address my urgent physical needs, and it was going to be performed by the best doctors I could find in my local community. But before that decision, I had also thought about seeking treatment from highly reputable health care facilities regionally and nationally. It seemed highly likely to me that these institutions would be able to provide some of the best experts specializing in the treatment of head and neck cancer. However, proximity to home was important to me in several ways: during recovery, I wanted to be near my loved ones and friends. I also had to consider the fact that I would be seeing oncologists in some capacity for the rest of my life. Getting on a plane or driving for three hours or more for a doctor's appointment would not work for me. In the end, I chose doctors I felt I could trust and who were close to my home.

It was on one of those pre-op days that I realized that I needed to get my mind off the upcoming surgery. So I visited the local zoo with a good friend. I think that it was no coincidence that we spent a long time observing elephants, one of the world's strongest animals. On this day, the God of all creation reminded me that He is stronger than the elephants that He Himself created. When I think about strength, the story of David and the Philistine giant, Goliath, comes to mind. David defeated the giant not because of his strength, confidence, or weapons (1 Samuel 17:1–58). Rather, he knew that God was his strength and defense. Like David, I was going to need to battle this cancer with God's abundant power (Psalm 147:5).

Furthermore, without God, we can do nothing. If we believe that we can do all things through Christ who strengthens us (Philippians 4:13), He will equip us with the strength to fight our battles and conquer any challenge we face. There is no limit to God's power or to what He knows and does.

Reflect: What strength do you need today?

Prayer: Lord, You are mighty in power. Thank You for giving me the strength to carry on even when I feel like I have no strength left. Help me remember Your limitless strength to help me fight and conquer my battles. In Jesus's name, amen.

Ten

Joy Comes in the Morning

For his anger is but for a moment, and his favor is for a lifetime.
Weeping may tarry for the night, but joy comes with the morning.
Psalm 30:5

Two days before surgery, I celebrated Mother's Day by playing golf with my husband and soaking up as much sunshine as possible before the big day. It was a perfectly sunny and warm day in the Sonoran Desert. After golfing, we invited the family over to share together in a take-out dinner. The next day, tempers flared, and emotions ran high among the family. A senseless argument broke out between my husband and the children. It broke my already fragile heart into pieces, and it seemed like everything was falling apart. Before going to bed, my niece, an ordained minister, called me on the phone and prayed with me. This was exactly what I needed to speak peace to my heart, ease my pain, and prepare me for surgery. Tears streamed down my face when I finally laid my head on my pillow that night. In that dark, emotional night, my situation felt hopeless. I was able to open my Bible and read Psalm 30:5, part of which says, "Weeping may tarry for the night, but joy comes with the morning." I could not even think about joy in this situation. Dr. Charles Stanley, pastor and preacher, explains today's verse like this: "When darkness covers your heart, you think you have no hope, but just as the sun disperses the nighttime at daybreak, your circumstances will change at the Lord's command."

It is sometimes difficult to find joy in our most trying circumstances, but Paul tells us we can rejoice in the Lord at all times (Philippians 4:4). It is the kind of joy that is Holy Spirit-inspired, that tells us that everything is going to be okay. This joy supersedes our circumstances. We can experience this joy in thinking about God's presence in us, His unconditional love, and His peace when we are dealing with dark nights and difficult circumstances like family conflicts, cancer pain, or any combination of adversities. He promises to bring joy, hope, and light in the morning.

"Sometimes God will isolate you before He elevates you. You may think that everything is falling apart, but actually everything is falling into place." —Unknown

Reflect: What difficulty and pain are you going through right now? How can you reset your thinking to rely more on God's strength instead of your own?

Prayer: Lord, today I will choose to find joy in You, even when I do not feel happy. Help me to remember that weeping will be replaced with laughter and pain with joy. In Jesus's name, amen.

Eleven

All We Need

> *Now to him who is able to do far more abundantly than all that we ask or think, according to the power at work within us.*
>
> *Ephesians 3:20*

The big day arrived. My cancer surgery was lengthy (over twelve hours) because it consisted of the surgical removal of the parotid gland followed by the reconstruction of my face and neck. The procedure, known as an anterolateral free flap, or ALT flap, was performed like an organ transplant. It involved removing healthy muscle tissue, along with its nerves and blood vessels, from the front of my left thigh and then implanting them into the right side of my face. The aim was to fill the hole that was expected once the cancerous parotid gland was removed. In addition to this procedure, healthy tendon chewing muscles were transferred from my jaw to my cheek and lower lip to provide support and function for the paralyzed right side of my face. This was intended to create facial symmetry and allow active facial motion, such as smiling. The final procedure during the reconstruction was the placement of a small platinum weight in the upper eyelid of my right eye to help the eyelid close completely.

Meanwhile, my family and friends all over the country were praying and waiting all day to get news about the completion of my surgery. When I was taken to the recovery room around 10:30 that night, I was covered in bandages and drainage tubes on my neck and left leg. God blessed me with yet another miracle because I woke up from this extremely complex and lengthy cancer surgery. I was still too groggy at the time to think of all the ways God's hands were supplying all that I needed. Upon reflecting, however, I realized that all the medical procedures, equipment, hospital, and, most certainly, a highly skilled medical team were His handpicked provisions for me. And moreover, He provided the loving support and prayers of loved ones. I was overjoyed for the abundance of grace, mercy, and strength He had allowed me to have in order to get through this ordeal triumphantly.

I could not have done this alone, and neither can you, whatever you may be facing or will face on your journey. It is God's power and the power of the Holy Spirit at work within us that allow us to do more than we can ever imagine. And because of His great love for us, He promises to give us everything we need far more abundantly than all that we may ask or think (Ephesians 3:20). God is able.

Reflect: What are your needs today? When have you been able to see God's power working through your weakness?

Prayer: Lord, thank You for Your grace and that You can do exceedingly above all that I ask or think. Help me to rely on Your power within me to get me through any challenge and to do Your will. In Jesus's name, amen.

Twelve

Strawberry Jell-O

> *Now the house of Israel called its name manna. It was like coriander seed, white, and the taste of it was like wafers made with honey.*
> *Exodus 16:31*

When I was waking up from general anesthesia, I looked up and saw very bright lights and nurses robed in dark blue scrubs fussing over me. I was happy to see my husband and children, who were very thankful that I had made it through alive. I think I can relate to how they must have felt waiting it out while I was separated from them in an unconscious state for over twelve hours. But to me, it seemed like a few minutes. One nurse asked me if I knew where I was and the current date. I recognized that I was in the hospital and it was May 16th. I still do not know why I was anxious to know the time of day. I was shocked when the nurse said it was 10:30 p.m. Another miracle: not only was I awake, but I was still in my right mind.

After I was transferred to the ICU, I felt groggy, hungry, and thirsty. The ICU nurse helped me sip water with a straw, and then I vomited immediately. Sometime during the night, I was feeling hungry. I asked the nurse for food. "We don't have much to eat on this floor except for strawberry or orange Jell-O. Would you like that?" she offered. I accepted the strawberry-flavored one. Looking back, I am amused at my desperation for food. You see, normally, I would never eat Jell-O, but I could not refuse it that night. This nurse spoon-fed me the Jell-O, and it satisfied my hunger. The Jell-O was like manna from heaven. Manna is the food God sent to the Israelites during their forty years in the desert (Exodus 16). David Guzik's commentary on Exodus 16 describes how God may provide from resources that we never knew existed. God provides for us because He has promised to do so, and He has the power to get it done. God gave everyone enough manna to satisfy their physical and spiritual hunger and to perform their daily activities. And Scripture says the manna tasted like wafers made with honey (Exodus 16:31).

Just as our physical body yearns for food and beverages, our spirit also has an appetite as well. To satisfy our spiritual hunger, we must eat the right spiritual food to obtain sustenance. This means "setting our mind on the things that are above" (Colossian 3:2) by spending time reading, studying, meditating on the Word of God, praying, listening to uplifting music, or other activities that turn our hearts toward God. We would not neglect our physical hunger. Therefore, we should not neglect our spiritual hunger, which only God and the indwelling Holy Spirit can satisfy. Eating the right spiritual food will build our faith muscles and give us spiritual energy.

Reflect: What are you doing to satisfy your spiritual hunger?

Prayer: Lord, thank You for Your daily provisions and for supplying all my needs, whether spiritual, physical, or emotional. Help me to feed on Your Word daily for my nourishment, strength, and growth. In Jesus's name, amen.

Thirteen

Clay Jars

> *O Israel, can I not do to you as this potter has done to his clay? As*
> *the clay is in the potter's hand, so are you in my hand.*
> *Jeremiah 18:6, NLT*

The first day after cancer surgery, the doctor told me that he removed all the visible cancer. I was hurting on the outside and inside. I felt like I had been run over by a semitrailer truck or badly beaten up after a boxing match and was broken into a thousand pieces, physically and mentally. My body was filled with so much anesthesia and pain medication. But for some reason, my mind wandered back to a time earlier in the year when I watched a friend, a skilled potter, make clay bowls using a pottery wheel. That day, I learned that while the potter is patiently turning the lump of clay on the pottery wheel, it can be fashioned precisely only when sitting in the center of the wheel. If the clay shifts off-center, then its shape becomes crooked and must be remolded. Also, the clay can crack or break during the molding process.

I definitely felt just like a clay bowl that was broken in pieces. The psalmist writes in Psalm 31:12 of feeling like he had "become like a broken vessel.". And as I pause to reflect on this verse, I am reminded of a fascinating Japanese art called *kintsugi*. This type of art that requires putting broken pottery pieces back together with gold is built on the idea that by embracing flaws and imperfections, you can create an even stronger, more beautiful piece of art. God is continually mending our broken hearts by using our trials and challenges to mold us and shape us into the people He wants us to be. While God is molding, refining, and shaping the clay in His hands, He is making us stronger in our faith and more beautiful every day, no matter how broken or fragile we are. God, the master potter, knows exactly what kind of clay bowl we are meant to become. We can learn from the prophet Jeremiah, whom God directed to watch the potter at work: "The clay is in the potter's hand, so are you in my hand" (Jeremiah 18:6).

Reflect: In what ways is God molding you?

Prayer: Dear Lord, thank You for molding and making me who You want me to be. In moments of weakness, please help to remember that You have placed a treasure in me that will strengthen me. In Jesus's name, amen.

Fourteen

Speechless

And the Holy Spirit helps us in our weakness. For example, we don't know what God wants us to pray for. But the Holy Spirit prays for us with groanings that cannot be expressed in words. And the Father who knows all hearts knows what the Spirit is saying, for the Spirit pleads for us believers in harmony with God's own will.

Romans 8:26–27, NLT

While I was in the ICU after the cancer surgery, it was difficult to pray and sleep. I could not express words of adoration, confession, thanksgiving, or supplication to God. In other words, I did not know how to communicate with God. The blood pulsating in my right ear was louder than the thoughts in my mind. There were constant beeping sounds coming from the monitors, checking my heart rate, blood pressure, oxygen level, and other vitals. On the first night, I kept hearing voices in the distance, and it felt like I was floating in bed. Perhaps I was hallucinating from all the pain medication that my body was receiving. Then, in the wee hours of the morning, a nurse came to draw blood. Soon after that, a parade of medical professionals came to check the flap (the transplant of tissue from my thigh to my face), using a device called an acoustic doppler sonogram. This device uses a doppler effect, that is, it emits ultrasound waves to detect changes in blood flow within the flap. It then generates a sound that is proportional to the flap's blood flow. The flap required critical and constant monitoring (every hour) for the early detection of vascular problems following surgery. I understood the importance of the monitoring, but this constant interruption left me exhausted and overwhelmed. I simply did not have the strength or words to go to God in prayer.

However, I felt the presence of God in the room. So I quietly asked, "God, please help me!" He reminded me that the Holy Spirit, who dwells within me, is my partner and guide. We receive the Holy Spirit when we accept Jesus as our savior (Acts 2:38). When we do not know what to say or cannot bring ourselves to find the right words to say, we are assured that the Holy Spirit will pray with us and for us in our weakness. That is exactly what the apostle Paul is sharing in today's verses (Romans 8:26–27). The Holy Spirit intercedes before God for us in harmony with God's own will for our lives. Therefore, we can confidently rest in the knowledge of this: "And we know that for those who love God, all things work together for good, for those who are called according to his purpose" (Romans 8:28). In his book *How to Let God Solve Your Problems*, Dr. Charles Stanley writes, "We may not see the evidence, but He is active and knows exactly what to do so that we have His best interest in the future."

Reflect: Think of a time when you did not know what to pray. How did you feel?

Prayer: Lord, You are holy. Thank You for the indwelling Holy Spirit.

Help me to remember that the Holy Spirit and Jesus are praying for me when I do not have the words. In Jesus's name, amen.

Fifteen

The Mirror

It seemed like I was in ICU forever, but it was only the third day. I had no idea how I looked since there was no mirror in the hospital room. Days later, when I was able to get out of bed and go to the bathroom, I looked at myself in the mirror, and I could not recognize the person I saw. I resembled a monster from a horror movie. The right side of my face was extremely swollen with a bandage over my right eye, and I had a fold along my right cheek and incisions behind my ears extending down the right side of my neck. There was not much I could do about what I was seeing in the mirror.

A mirror is useful for evaluating ourselves. However, spending time looking in the mirror can only reflect what is physically there, not what is below the surface. The wall mirror was giving me a true perspective and a physical reflection of my scars and imperfections, not a spiritual reflection of my soul. Did you know there is a mirror for the soul? That mirror is God's truth, written in the Bible. James tells us that God's Word in the Bible is like a mirror: "For the word of God is alive and powerful. It is sharper than the sharpest two-edged sword, cutting between soul and spirit, between joint and marrow. It exposes our innermost thoughts and desires" (Hebrews 4:12, NLT). Just as a mirror reflects what we look like on the outside, God's Word reflects what we are like inside. This is the reflection that God always sees—a true reflection into our soul, our hearts, and the image of who we truly are.

When we use God's Word as a mirror, it shows us how we can become more like God, how much God loves us (Colossians 3:12). It also shows us that we are God's masterpiece, a work of art (Ephesians 2:10). When we intently and truthfully look in the mirror of God's Word, we can "humbly accept the word planted in [our] hearts" (James 1:21, NLT), and we will see ourselves as God sees us. After all, God's truth is the only mirror that matters.

Reflect: Using God's Word as a mirror, what does it show you? Does it show you what you need to change? Does it show you how to live in the power of God?

Prayer: Lord, we thank You for seeing us for who we are and what we can become when we obey Your Word. Please help us to truthfully look in Your mirror and obey Your Word. In Jesus's name, amen.

Sixteen

Trust in God

Trust in the Lord with all your heart, and do not lean on your own understanding. In all your ways acknowledge him and he will make straight your paths.
Proverbs 3:5–6

I was grateful for each day and for whatever progress I was making post-surgery. I knew that this journey required patience and faith for me to be well again. However, the challenges were coming in all shapes and sizes. For instance, I found that the hospital food was neither appetizing nor nutritious. This included the various flavors of protein shakes that were loaded with sugar. The nutritionist in me told me that I was missing many important nutrients like potassium, phosphorus, and magnesium. I was given dietary supplements for most of these minerals. However, iron was not included. Within a couple days, my blood iron level dropped way below the expected range, which meant that I was anemic. The attending physician told me that I needed a blood transfusion to increase my low iron level, which more than likely stemmed from blood loss during surgery. In any case, the idea of receiving a blood transfusion became concerning, even though I knew that they are typically safe. I expressed my anxiety about this procedure to the nurse on duty because I knew about possible complications during this process. What if the blood being used was contaminated? What if my body rejected this blood? Then what?

Before I knew it, I was back in the driver's seat of this journey, but I yielded and did what had kept me safe thus far: I prayed to God that everything would go well and left the outcome to Him. I trusted Him to take the lead, just as He had for that life-changing twelve-hour surgery now behind me. Then, before the procedure started, the nurse reassured me that during the process, she would be observing signs and symptoms and monitoring my vital signs periodically. If there were any complications, she would stop the transfusion immediately. Four hours later, it was completed successfully. I sought God's help in this process, and He answered my prayer (Psalm 34:4). I am still learning how to give up my seat to Him. I trust Him with all my heart. To depend on Him and not on what I know about certain things, like the transfusion process. God will direct our path, but we must do our part, which is to acknowledge and trust Him to lead the way in all of our circumstances. Yielding to God's control is no small act, but I believe that is the only way we can truly say that we trust Him completely (Proverbs 3:5–6).

In moments like these, we must put and keep our trust in the invisible God, who never stops working and sustains all things.

Reflect: Think about a time when you trusted in God and relied on His guidance. How did this affect your decisions and the outcomes of the situation?

Prayer: Lord, thank You that I can place my trust in You. Please help me to trust You with all my heart and to not lean not on my own understanding. In Jesus's name, amen.

Seventeen

The Doctor and the Nurse

> *But you, Lord, are a compassionate and gracious God, slow to anger, abounding in love and faithfulness.*
> *Psalm 86:15, NIV*

The whole time that I was in the ICU at the hospital, the medical team checked in on me several times a day every day. When the ENT surgeon came to see me on the first day after surgery, he asked, "How is your family doing?" He continued by saying, "You went through a lot, and they did too!"

His question became etched in my mind, even though I still felt badly beaten up. It was almost as if he or one of his family members had experienced the pain and trauma I felt as a cancer patient. I recognized the same compassionate connection in an ICU nurse who shared my beliefs as a Christian. She was a young nurse who was the age of my youngest son. She ensured that I always felt comfortable and spent time intentionally listening to me as I spoke about my husband and my children. She sought to understand my heartaches and pain. I was deeply touched by the compassion the doctor and the nurse showed me.

God placed a compassionate doctor and nurse in my life to comfort me during this painful time. They went beyond their duty or obligation to serve. We can trust in God's power to provide people in our path to help us when we pass through adversity. And sometimes, we are the ones who God provides to others to help in their time of need. It is often said that compassion springs from adversity—because of our experiences, we can empathize with others. The psalmist reminds us that God himself is "compassionate and gracious" (Psalm 86:15). His immeasurable compassion, love, and faithfulness are always there for all of us.

The life of Jesus is our best example of compassion. But what is compassion? According to the Cambridge dictionary, compassion is "a strong feeling of sympathy and sadness for other people's suffering." Matthew, a disciple of Jesus, tells us that "When [Jesus] saw the crowds, he had compassion on them, because they were confused and helpless, like sheep without a shepherd" (Matthew 9:36, NLT). Then later in chapter 14, Matthew again shows us that Jesus also "had compassion on them and healed their sick" (Matthew 14:14). Furthermore, it was because He cared deeply for all humanity that Jesus did the ultimate by dying in our place to save us from eternal death. So as we face each new day, we can be assured of his ever-present, unfailing compassion, which are new each morning (Lamentations 3:22–23, NIV).

Reflect: How has God shown compassion in your own life or the life of a loved one with a health challenge?

Prayer: Heavenly Father, thank You for being gracious and compassionate. Help me to fill my heart with the compassion of Jesus so that I can have compassion for others. In Jesus's name, amen.

Eighteen

Count Your Blessings

> *Bless the Lord, O my soul, and forget not all his benefits, who*
> *forgives all your iniquity, who heals all your diseases.*
> *Psalm 103:2–3*

My hospital stay had come to an end on the sixth day following cancer surgery. Upon my release, I received prescription medication for pain and instructions on how to take care of the wounds on my neck and thigh. It certainly felt great to be back in the comfort of my home again, but honestly, it felt a little scary because I was no longer receiving around-the-clock care from a medical team. I quickly realized that I would not be able to take care of myself for a while. The independence that I enjoyed all my life around self-care would now need to be shelved. I needed to rely on my family and friends who were eagerly waiting to help me in whatever way they could, from helping with wound dressing to combing my hair, helping with baths, meals, laundry, and keeping me entertained. They did all they could to bring me cheer and help me smile again. It was clear that they would be there for me, no matter what it took. Without a doubt, I cannot imagine what it would have been like without the love and support of my family and friends throughout this journey.

There were so many blessings I was thankful for, and as I penned my thoughts today, I recall singing the song "Count Your Blessings" when I was a child: "Count your many blessings, name them one by one. Count your many blessings, see what God has done. Count your blessings, name them one by one. Count your many blessings and see what God has done." God gives us a great abundance of blessings (Luke 6:38), and He continues to bless us with things that we have not even asked for. Sometimes the devil tries to let us forget about these blessings, especially when we are facing adversity. However, we must not be deceived, for God is good all the time; He fills our lives with good things (Psalm 103:5, NLT), and He is the source of every good and perfect gift (James 1:17). Instead of focusing on your current situation, remember "all his benefits" (Psalm 103:2). Be intentional about writing out each blessing God gives you every day while thanking Him for these blessings.

Reflect: What blessings from God are you thankful for today?

Prayer: Thank You for all Your blessings, wisdom, and understanding that You have enriched me with. Help me to remember all Your blessings in my life. Please endow me with all the abundance of blessings that You give me daily. In Jesus's name, amen.

Nineteen

How Long?

Two weeks after surgery, I had my first follow-up visit with all the
doctors. I finally asked the ENT surgeon, "What is the prognosis?"

"It's hard to know with this unusual type of cancer," he responded.
He stated matter-of-factly, "Every patient is different, and your case
is very unique." He told me that the cancerous parotid gland tumor
needed more extensive testing to further classify the type and sub-
type of this rare form of cancer. By then, I was getting stronger, and
I had much more time on my hands, so I did some research on the
survival rate of parotid gland cancer. I discovered that there is very
limited survival rate information available for people with parotid
gland cancer, especially for ethnic minorities (mixed African, Euro-
pean, and Caribbean descent) like me. It is well known that cultural
and racial diversity have not been equally represented in a vast

number of clinical studies. With limited data for ethnic minorities with parotid gland cancer, it is difficult to predict the survival rate. In addition, according to the experts, the statistics on parotid gland cancer are not very accurate since there are multiple factors that make a difference one way or another.

When we are facing a life-threatening illness, we often want to know how long we will live. The truth is that no one knows for sure how much time we have on earth. The Bible makes it clear that our days are numbered and the length of our lives are determined by God (Job 14:5, NIV). Only He can give us an expiration date because He knows the exact number of days, seconds, hours, and minutes of human life. When we know God, we can say with the psalmist, "My times are in your hand" (Psalm 31:15). He will give us exactly what we need until our last day on earth.

It is important to remember that doctors and clinical trial data can only give us an educated guess. We must live our lives to the fullest. Make peace with those who may have wronged you and make memories that will comfort those you leave behind.

Reflect: How are you spending your days? Are you making good memories?

Prayer: Lord, it is easy to believe that I can somehow control my own lifespan, but You determine the length of my days. Help me to be a good steward of the time You have allotted me. In Jesus's name, amen.

Twenty

Time Alone

> *You keep him in perfect peace whose mind is stayed on you, because he trusts in you.*
> *Isaiah 26:3*

It was the beginning of June in the Sonoran Desert. The evening sunsets and star-filled skies in the desert remind me of God's splendor, how big He is, and how small I am. I thought about heaven when the setting sun on the horizon turned the sky into a painting of hues of orange, yellow, and pink. It was unusually cool on this early summer evening as I sat outside on my patio. A gentle wind was blowing through the mesquite trees as I watched the owl swoop down and perch on the electric pole. The sounds of coyotes were howling in the distance. In this time alone, I welcomed God into my presence, and I asked Him to quiet my mind so that I could hear His voice clearly. I wanted to connect on a deeper level. He told me to let go of my worries, relax, and look upon my life as a gift. By the end of the evening, God had given me the kind of "peace which surpasses all understanding" (Philippians 4:7, NIV), and it was not the peace "as the world gives" (John 14:27). In his book *Overcomer*, Dr. David Jeremiah writes that the peace God offers is "a calm, unafraid, unruffled confidence that, having placed our lives in His hands, all will be well."

I was not always at peace throughout this cancer journey. Before the diagnosis, when I was waiting for the results from the biopsy and waiting for surgery, I was very anxious. I fluctuated between having God's peace and becoming filled with fear about my health status. I wondered how I could preserve God's peace in my heart and mind as I moved forward on the rest of my journey. I discovered that I must "let the peace of Christ rule in your hearts, since, as members of one body, you were called to peace. And be thankful" (Colossians 3:15).

Spending time alone with God, meditating on His Word, praying, and keeping our minds on Him (Isaiah 26:3) are good stepping stones to finding peace daily. Meditation on God's Word for me is like having a meal—chewing on His words and digesting them in my mind throughout the day. Our minds are constantly filled with so many distractions that God is telling us to keep our thoughts on Him and to take hold of His peace that surpasses all understanding. We cannot obtain this kind of peace on our own.

Reflect: How can you spend more time alone with God to experience His peace?

Prayer: Lord, thank You for Your peace, which surpasses all understanding. Help me to spend more time alone, meditating on Your Word, and praying, especially during challenging times. In Jesus's name, amen.

Twenty-One

Behind the Mask

With more ability to move around after cancer surgery, I could now venture out to the grocery store, coffee shop, and other public places. But before visiting these places, I had another obstacle to overcome on this journey, and that was my physical appearance. I was not comfortable with my look, and my worst fear was that everyone would be staring and judging my appearance. What if I ran into somebody I knew? Then that meant I would have to explain what happened to me. Awkward! I was not mentally prepared for that encounter. On my first outing to the neighborhood grocery store, I wore one of those N95 masks made popular by the pandemic. The mask was a great deflector for me. People would be forced to look directly into my eyes instead of the other parts of my face. One morning, after wearing the mask for several days, I looked in the mirror and said, "Okay, God. This is my face that I must live with. I cannot wear a mask forever; let's get on with life." So I went to the grocery store without wearing a mask. I came to the realization that what I was doing was living in fear.

Fear can paralyze us and stop us from living the abundant life God provides for us. Fear of circumstances and things around us and fear of what may or may not happen are not from God. The Bible tells us that God has not given us a spirit of fear but of power, love, and self-control (2 Timothy 1:7). When David, a young shepherd boy, defeated the Philistine giant Goliath, he did not let fear get a hold of him (1 Samuel 17:1–58). David was victorious because he placed his trust in God, knowing that God was more powerful than his fears. The psalmist writes in Psalm 56:11, "In God I trust; I shall not be afraid. What can man do to me?"

It is easy to become overwhelmed with fear, which often lurks in the shadows, waiting for the right moment to attack. The key to overcoming fear is refusing to give in to it and trusting God for every outcome.

Reflect: What would it look like if you let the power and love and self-control of God take over instead of fear?

Prayer: Dear God, thank You for giving me a spirit of power, love, and self-control to face any challenge. Help me trust You to help me to overcome any fear or anxiety that may come upon me. In Jesus's name, amen.

Twenty-Two

A Shield

> *But you, O Lord, are a shield about me. My glory, and the lifter of my head.*
> *Psalm 3:3*

My husband and I met with a radiation oncologist three weeks after surgery to discuss and outline the benefits and side effects of the radiation treatment that I would be receiving over the next six weeks. Some of these side effects included dry mouth, fatigue, burning of the skin in and around the treatment area, and taste alteration. The job of the radiation oncologist was to make sure that the amount of radiation I would be receiving was the appropriate amount and administered in the right area as well as to monitor my progress during treatment. The attending team of experts also explained that the goal of the radiation therapy (also called radio-therapy) was to kill any remaining microscopic cancer cells that may still be hanging around in my face and neck area post-surgery. This would minimize the risk of cancer recurrence. Before starting radiation therapy, a mask covering my face and shoulders would first be created. This see-through mask, made from a kind of light blue plastic mesh, was created specifically for me to fit my face and over my shoulder. It was to be worn for every radiotherapy treatment. There would be a total of thirty-three high-dose radiation therapy treatments, five times per week, with each one lasting about five to ten minutes. Every day that I went for therapy, I laid down on a table, then a nurse would fit the mask over my face and shoulders and then snap it down to the table. I could not move my head, neck, or shoulders at any time during radiotherapy. Thus, the mask is designed to restrain my head so that the radiation targets the exact same spots (down to the millimeter) at every radiation treatment.

The first radiation therapy session was completely painless. However, being strapped down on a table gave me a great deal of anxiety. In those moments, I knew that God was protecting me. Just like this mask was a shield used to make sure the radiation only targeted the designated location of the tissues in my face and neck, so was God my shield over my heart and mind. As a shield, He offers protection and defense during our difficult times. When David was being pursued by enemies, he was certain that the Lord was "a shield about me, my glory, and the lifter of my head" (Psalm 3:3). David envisioned God protecting him from his enemies like a shield protects a warrior from arrows, darts, swords, and spears. The Lord sustained him and protected David from his enemies.

When difficulties arise, it is good to remember that God is a shield around us. By knowing God's Word intimately and standing on it, we can always be assured that we already have this same protection.

Reflect: How can God be your shield today even if you are not currently facing a difficult situation?

Prayer: Lord, thank You that You are a shield around me. Help me to trust Your protection and remain hopeful during difficult times. In Jesus's name, amen.

Twenty-Three

Don't Worry

> *Don't worry about anything; instead, pray about everything. Tell God what you need, and thank him for all he has done. Then you will experience God's peace, which exceeds anything we can understand. His peace will guard your hearts and minds as you live in Christ Jesus.—Philippians 4:6–7, NLT*

I learned from various reputable sources that there are many adverse effects of radiation therapy. In general, radiation is extremely toxic to the body. Not only would it kill or slow the growth of cancer cells in my face and neck area, but it would also affect all the healthy cells nearby. Although this type of treatment is supposed to be beneficial, it could affect my quality of life in the long term. For example, radiation to the head and neck area increases the risk of tooth decay and oral infection due to a decrease in saliva production and damage to tooth structure. Permanent or temporary loss of taste is another complication of radiation therapy. The taste buds are very sensitive to radiation. Given these possible outcomes,

I became worried about what might eventually happen to my health over time. While I sat worrying about these problems, I was making myself feel sick. In this moment, I did not think to "seek the Lord" (Isaiah 55:6) through prayer.

The word worry comes from an Old English term meaning "choke" or "strangle." In fact, that is exactly what worry does: it chokes us. Worry cannot control or change the future. Worrying is not productive and only messes up the present moment. In the apostle Paul's letter to the Philippians, he admonishes all believers to pray when they are worried. They should reject worry, ask God for what they need in every situation, thank Him for all the things He has already done in their lives, and rest knowing that God's peace is theirs (Philippians 4:6–7). God does not promise that He will change our circumstances or that our troubles will disappear; He promises to give us peace. In other words, God will change our inclination toward worry so that it does not cause us turmoil. It bears repeating that we cannot control the future, as hard as we may try, but we can certainly pray about it. The next time you have worries, give them all to God and let Him handle them. Search the scriptures on the topic of worry with the same determination we sometimes have in googling on the Internet. Then take every worry and add it to your prayer list.

Reflect: What worries can you turn into prayers today so that you can experience God's peace?

Prayer: Lord, help me to turn my worries into prayers, and I will pray with thanksgiving so that I can experience Your peace. In Jesus's name, amen.

Twenty-Four

Be Patient

After four weeks, the wound on my thigh was mostly healed, but the swelling and numbness on the right side of my face, neck, and shoulder remained. I continued to drink beverages using a straw to prevent drooling all over myself. I could not open my mouth wide enough to eat something like a hamburger. I predominantly chewed my food on the left side of my mouth, and I did it slowly. The feeling of pressure and heaviness in my right ear were also still present, and I had a lopsided smile. Other physical challenges were also noticeable, like when I sat on the passenger side of the car and the seat belt irritated my neck and shoulder. I could also not lift my right arm above my head and therefore had difficulty getting dressed or combing my hair. At the follow-up visit, the ENT surgeon had told me that numbness on the right side of my face may never go away but that the swelling would go down, especially after the completion of radiation treatment. The surgeon also told me the numbness and stiffness in the neck and shoulder would feel better with physical therapy. The facial plastic surgeon (one of the attending physicians from my surgery) had reassured me that it would take several months, or maybe even a year, to get a full smile, though not the smile I had before the facial paralysis.

I began to doubt whether these doctors were being honest with me. So I asked my husband, "Do you think the swelling will go down like the doctors said?" He responded immediately, saying, "You need to trust the process. Be patient." I wanted to see the changes occur immediately. But healing was going to take a long time. I had no choice but to wait. It seemed like I had forgotten all the months I had waited for a cancer diagnosis or the many days and nights for the results of lab tests and scans.

Waiting can be hard. Most of us would prefer quick answers and results right away that would free us from pain or difficulties. We must wait for the unseen seed buried in the ground to sprout, plants to grow, children to mature into adults, answers to prayers, dreams to come true, and maybe even a new season for our favorite streaming program. All these things require patience. King David waited for a very long time to be king and to be rescued from his enemies, one of whom was his own son, Absalom. When you read his story, he did not always trust the process, and while in the process of waiting, he wrote many of the psalms in the Bible. King David trusted God and advises us to "wait patiently on the Lord." Being brave and courageous takes unwavering confidence undergirded with patience.

Reflect: What thing is requiring your patience right now?

Prayer: Lord, thank You that You are working all things out for my good. Help me to patiently wait for You, no matter what I am dealing with. In Jesus's name, amen.

Twenty-Five

Confidence

> *Such is the confidence that we have through Christ toward God.*
> *Not that we are sufficient in ourselves to claim anything as coming*
> *from us, but our sufficiency is from God.*
> 2 Corinthians 3:4–5

Before starting radiation therapy, I had reached out to several members of my family and friends to ask about their experiences with various cancer treatments, such as radiation and chemotherapy. There was only one person who had ever received radiation treatment while a few of the others had done chemotherapy. They shared with me the symptoms they experienced with each kind of treatment, like nausea and vomiting, fatigue, burned skin, mouth sores, and a metallic taste in the mouth. Some told me that my skin would get burned and turn very dark, and there was nothing that could be done to prevent it from happening. This all sounded very frightening, but overall, the information they shared helped me prepare for what I might expect with the upcoming treatment.

Their advice also helped me build up my confidence and courage to overcome some of my fears about radiation therapy. My confidence level had been wearing thin as I became increasingly uncertain about whether I could withstand the high amounts of radiation that my body would receive. The frustration and fear of facing this challenge seemed too big for me to handle. But through a quiet whisper from within, God gently reminded me that I needed to depend on His strength to find my confidence. I recalled the time I first became a mother. I was both scared and unprepared, and I thought that I was inadequate for motherhood when I brought my baby girl home. Happily, I became a mother two more times, building up my confidence level as a mother. The apostle Paul reassures us that although situations in our lives can cause us to doubt our capabilities, we can always find an unlimited supply of grace, strength, and confidence by trusting in the Lord (2 Corinthians 3:4–5). By humbling ourselves and calling upon the sufficiency of God, we can face every inadequacy or difficult situation with fearless confidence. It is the Holy Spirit's enabling, matched with our spiritual gifts, talents, and abilities, that help us build this confidence.

Reflect: How is God strengthening you to face every situation with His confidence?

Prayer: Lord, thank You that our confidence is not in ourselves but in Christ. Remind me that I need to depend on Your strength to find confidence. In Jesus's name, amen.

Twenty-Six

A Season

I had finally begun radiation therapy about five weeks after surgery. Within the first week of therapy, I experienced nausea and a dry mouth. The following week, I lost my desire to eat. Food that I had always enjoyed, like chocolate, was tasteless. As a matter of fact, most food either tasted like nothing or left a bitter or metallic taste in my mouth. Also noticeable was that my taste preferences for various foods were changing daily. The radiation oncologist assured me, "Eventually, you will regain your taste after radiation is done." He encouraged me to eat foods that I had never eaten. I took his advice and tried a different food every day, like chocolate hummus, which tasted horrible! I was thinking that for me to even know it was horrible, my taste buds still had some hope left.

By the third week of therapy, I had completely lost what little appetite I had left, and I constantly felt nauseous. Nausea puts a damper on everything! With the advice of the nutritionist at the cancer center, I started using medical marijuana in the form of orange-tasting gummies to increase my appetite and reduce my nausea. When I did not feel like eating, I forced myself to consume food, even if it tasted bad. I began experimenting with new ideas for food preparation, like seasoning meat with different spices and herbs that I did not typically use. This helped me to enjoy food a little bit more. I knew all too well that I needed to "Let food be thy medicine and medicine be thy food." This often-quoted phrase spoken by Hippocrates signifies that the nutrients from food control almost every function of the body and mind while revitalizing our health.

Thus, I longed for the day when my appetite would return to normal, when I would begin to enjoy eating the food I once loved and benefit from the nutrition that my body so desperately needed. This journey with cancer that had come upon me so suddenly and altered every aspect of my life was not only very challenging, but it seemed at times like there was no chance of normalcy in my life ever again. But one of the things I learned is that I could look at the ups and downs of this journey as a season of life. More importantly, by God's grace, I would get through it. Ecclesiastes 3:1 explains that "For everything there is a season, a time for every matter under heaven." The remaining verses of this chapter further teach us that there is a time to be born and to die, to plant and harvest, to break down and build up, and to mourn and laugh (Ecclesiastes 3:2–4). Throughout this passage, King Solomon reminds us that we will always be in seasons that are changing, but God has arranged the details of our lives within each season, and He is guiding us. We will have good and bad seasons and easy seasons and hard ones, but we can trust that God is in control of everything that happens in all our seasons throughout this life.

Reflect: Do you place your trust in God in all seasons?

Prayer: Father, thank You for guiding me through the seasons of my life. Help me to trust You and set my eyes on You during the hard seasons. In Jesus's name, amen.

Twenty-Seven

Our Burden

> *Come to me, all who labor and are heavy laden, and I will give you rest. Take my yoke upon you, and learn from me, for I am gentle and lowly in heart, and you will find rest for your souls. For my yoke is easy, and my burden is light.*
> Matthew 11:28–30

"You are halfway there," my friend reminded me. I had completed almost three weeks of the six weeks of radiation therapy. At this point in the journey, the weight of everything that I had endured with surgery and radiation treatments thus far was beginning to press heavily on my heart and mind. I was facing various family challenges while also feeling extremely anxious about the probability of a recurrence of cancer and, of course, the possible short-term and long-term effects of radiation treatment. These were the burdens that I was carrying around on my shoulders as I traveled on this cancer journey.

I felt burdened beyond what I knew I could handle. My heart

was heavy and full. I came to realize that I really needed a person to talk to, so I sought a therapist. In my book *Practical Ways to Better Mental Health*, I wrote that a counselor or therapist will most likely have the skills to help us build our "mental muscle," just like a personal trainer can do with muscles in our body. And God knew exactly who to send me—a godly therapist in my time of need. Her encouraging words and emotional support helped me to navigate my struggles and sort through my feelings.

It is not easy to let go of our burdens. Our shoulders were never meant to carry the weight of the world on them. When we find ourselves carrying heavy burdens, it is important to reach out to professionals who may help us determine behaviors we need to change. As a believer, I need to remember that I do not need to carry the weights of my burdens because God promises to "daily bear our burden" (Psalm 68:19, NIV), and His promises are always true. He comes alongside us every day to bear all our struggles. He sends people (in my case, a therapist or an oncologist) across our path to become instruments that He can use for our benefit. Once we have this help, we are better able to identify and offer each burden up to God and rest in His help. He is the one who provides us with rest (Matthew 11:28–30).

Reflect: How can you let God bear your burden?

Prayer: Lord, thank You for Your endless grace and love. Help me to release all the burdens that are weighing on my heart and mind. In Jesus's name, amen.

Twenty-Eight

Run with Endurance

<blockquote>

And let us run with endurance the race that is set before us. We do this by keeping our eyes on Jesus, the champion who initiates and perfects our faith.
Hebrews 12:1b–2a, NLT

</blockquote>

It was the fourth week of radiation therapy with two more weeks to go. The normally lightly colored skin on my neck and face had turned dark brown, like the color of dark chocolate. That area of my skin was also burned and peeling. There was ringing in my ears, slight chewing difficulty, and mild fatigue. Additionally, I still could not lift my right arm above my head, which resulted from an injury to nerves in my shoulder during the cancer removal surgery. Thus, it was a little challenging to comb my hair and reach for things sitting above my head. Despite these issues, I summoned up enough strength to go out each day for brisk walks with my dog. I now had enough mobility to start physical therapy treatments at least twice per week for my shoulder and neck. Physical therapy became a very important part of my recovery and rehabilitation.

There was always some degree of pain during the thirty to sixty minutes of physical therapy exercises that I performed daily. However, I tried to not allow pain to keep me from working through the rehabilitation process. My hunger for healing was greater than the pain. I felt like an athlete training for a competition during physical therapy. My physical therapist was my trainer, getting me prepared for my future activities with various strenuous exercise routines. It was important for me to get back to the outdoor activities, like playing tennis and golf, that I enjoyed doing before my cancer diagnosis. There was no way I was going to quit physical therapy sessions before my recovery was complete, no matter how long it took or how I was feeling physically. Athletes endure the suffering during training because they are focused on the goal. Our journey through life is also a race of life that God set before us, in which Jesus provides us with the strength we need by initiating and perfecting our faith by the power of the Holy Spirit. Not only is Jesus our ultimate trainer, but He is also our champion. Thus, we look to Him as we continue to train and receive the discipline that enables us to grow in faith. Any opposition, trials, or suffering we endure along the way are just part of the training. But to get to the goal, we must keep training and running. See Hebrews 12:1–4 for further insight on this teaching around life as a race.

Reflect: How can you persevere through the race God has set before you?

Prayer: Give me the strength to run with endurance and overcome any challenges that I may face. May I always remember that You are the author and perfecter of our faith. In Jesus's name we pray, amen.

Twenty-Nine

Soar Like an Eagle

> *But they who wait for the LORD shall renew their strength; they shall mount up with wings like eagles; they shall run and not be weary; they shall walk and not faint.*
> *Isaiah 40:31*

The adverse effects of radiation therapy were continuing to surface. One morning, as I was brushing my hair, I noticed clumps of hair in my hands. I looked closer in the mirror, and not surprisingly, a huge patch of hair was missing on the right side of my scalp around the same spot that the radiation was hitting. The thought of cutting all my hair off came to my mind. However, I was able to cover the patch by pulling my hair back in a ponytail. In addition to this latest challenge, I had intermittent pain in my shoulder and neck, loss of appetite, nausea, dry mouth, and chewing difficulties. But the mirror that morning that showed me the missing patch of hair also reminded me of the struggle I was having with the changes to my face—this amid awkward comments from others about beauty that only served to further deepen my emotional pain. My thoughts ran wild, and I felt as if no one understood what I was going through.

These dark thoughts and emotions about my health were pressing on my mind. I felt like I was in the "valley of the shadow of death," as David described in Psalm 23:4. That morning, tears flowed down my face, and I found myself sobbing uncontrollably. James Montgomery Boice, a Bible teacher and author, calls this "a combination of dark thoughts and uncontrollable emotions." He wrote that "when we no longer sense that God is blessing us, we tend to ruminate on our failures and get into an emotional funk." And when our emotions take over, it is always hard to get back on track. "This is because the best means of doing this—calm reflection and a review of past blessings—are being swept away." This was exactly how I felt. On this day, it took a lot of strength to pull myself out of this dark place mentally. Valleys are part of life, and some of us will be there at one time or another. Our experience in the valley is what prepares us for the mountaintop—to a place where we soar best.

In my moment of despair, I sought the Lord in prayer and told Him about my deepest concerns. He heard the cry of my heart, and He promised me that I would "mount up with wings like eagles" (Isaiah 40:31). What an incredible promise—one that He had made to the Israelites at a time when they were filled with hopelessness and fear while being held in captivity. The image of eagles—majestic creatures known for their strength and ability to soar through storms and soar way above the clouds—let us know that, like the Israelites, when we put our complete trust in God, we will receive renewed strength to withstand whatever storms come our way. We will soar on wings, just like the eagles.

Reflect: What practical steps can you take to renew your strength in God?

Prayer: Lord, thank You for Your unfailing love for me. May You renew my strength so that I can soar like an eagle when I am in despair. In Jesus's name, amen.

Thirty

This Too Shall Pass

For this light momentary affliction is preparing for us an eternal weight of glory beyond all comparison, as we look not to the things that are seen but to the things that are unseen. For the things that are seen are transient, but the things that are unseen are eternal.

2 Corinthians 4:17–18

It was almost the end of the six-week radiation therapy. I was incredibly exhausted mentally and physically while at the same time being relieved that this part of the journey was behind me. I had lost weight, some of my hair, my appetite, and my sense of taste. I was nauseous and fatigued, and my mouth was dry, mainly from the removal of my parotid gland (one of the main salivary glands). I still had intermittent pain in my shoulder and neck. I mentioned these issues to my mother, and she said, "This, too, shall pass." The radiation oncologist had used these same words a few weeks earlier when I discussed the symptoms I was experiencing. This popular expression, often used by people, is not explicitly found in the Bible.

The exact origin is unknown, but some seem to think it is a paraphrase of "and it came to pass," which occurs several hundred times in the King James Bible version. Others think it comes from a fable written by a Persian poet or is part of Jewish folklore.

Regardless of the origin of this phrase, I can look back at many of the challenges and troubles that I have faced a year ago or even over my lifetime. They have passed and are behind me. However, during the actual experience, it was not always easy to see how these challenges and troubles would ever pass. And some may never pass during our time here on earth. The apostle Paul knew this all too well. Drawing from his experiences of tremendous physical pain and emotional suffering, he provides us with a strategy in 2 Corinthians 4:17–18 to help us reshape our thinking by always keeping our focus on the prize of eternal glory, not on the trials and afflictions of this world that are light and momentary. Like a disciplined athlete who does not easily quit, we must train ourselves to allow the promise of the unseen, which is our eternal prize, to spur us on to victory. But we cannot do it alone; we need reinforcement. So we turn again to Paul as he reminds us in Ephesians 3:16 that God's Holy Spirit provides us with unlimited resources to empower us with inner strength. Yes, we need His strength for whatever giants we might face here on earth, reminding ourselves that they must pass.

Reflect: Where is your heart focused? Are you focused on things from God's perspective?

Prayer: God, thank You that my problems are temporary. Help me to remember that whatever I am going through will not last forever and that You have good things in store for the future. In Jesus's name, amen.

Thirty-One

Be Content

Not that I am speaking of being in need, for I have learned in whatever situation I am to be content. I know how to be brought low, and I know how to abound. In any and every circumstance, I have learned the secret of facing plenty and hunger, abundance and need.
Philippians 4:11–12

The final day of radiation came a few days before my birthday. It felt so good to have reached this point. I no longer needed to be snapped down to a radiation table with a mask fitted over my face and shoulder. After the last treatment, it is customary for cancer patients to ring a bell to symbolize the triumph over adversity and mark the end of the cancer treatment. After six long weeks of radiation treatment, I rang the little silver bell with joy. I was content with God's graciousness in giving me more time to enjoy life here on earth with family and friends and that He was with me on this journey.

What does it mean to be content? According to the Cambridge

dictionary, content is a "happy and satisfied feeling." The Bible describes true contentment as being satisfied with what we have, knowing God will never leave us or fail us (Hebrews 13:5) and delighting in His graciousness and sovereignty. I have come to realize that it is not possessions, beauty, fame, or earthly things that make us feel content and that these things could never produce true contentment. By nature, we may find it easy to be content when things are going our way. But the true measure of our contentment can only be known when a test comes along, our circumstances become difficult, or we feel broken because of sudden or prolonged adversities finding their way into our lives. When the apostle Paul wrote the words in the verses for today (Philippians 4:11–12), he was speaking from a place of experience. He had faced imprisonment, beatings, rejection, and all kinds of dangers, yet he learned to be content through his experiences.

Take notice that he *learned*. Paul could be content in whatever situation he was in because he practiced seeing his life from God's perspective; he had learned how to prioritize or concentrate on the eternal and not the temporal. Like Paul, adjusting our perspectives and priorities while looking to our source of power will strengthen our contentment level no matter what we may face or what God has allowed to come into our lives (2 Corinthians 12:8–10).

Reflect: In what ways can you learn to be content today?

Prayer: Lord, You are gracious. Thank You that all good and perfect things come from You. Please help me learn to be content in all things and to trust You for all I need. In Jesus's name, amen.

Thirty-Two

Guard Your Heart

> *Above all else, guard your heart, for everything you do flows from it.*
>
> *Proverbs 4:23, NIV*

It had been two weeks since radiation treatment ended. On this day, I decided to hold a pity party for myself. I still cannot believe that I attended the party, considering all that I have told you about my journey thus far. In any case, there I was, entertaining thoughts of every bad thing that had happened to me during this entire cancer journey thus far. I simply began to feel sorry for myself. Then I asked myself questions like "Will my taste return to normal? Will I lose any hearing in my right ear? Is the cancer completely gone? Where will the cancer show up next?" I felt sick and saddened just thinking about the cancer recurrence and all the other possible long-term effects of radiation. Sometime later, I told my good friend, "The doctor said the cancer is a high-grade carcinoma that is very aggressive. The doctor also said that the recurrence of cancer is very high. I am not optimistic about the prognosis."

She responded, saying, "You are being Eeyore." On that day, I was truly acting like the donkey Eeyore from the *Winnie the Pooh* story written by A.A. Milne in the 1920s. Eeyore is the negative character who is always sad and sees the dark side of everything. I was becoming negative and cynical, thinking only of the worst possible outcomes. My thought pattern was making me sicker within myself than I cared to admit.

The heart is the source of all our thoughts, attitudes, and behaviors. Our actions, behaviors, and speech flow from the heart. The heart that the Bible is talking about is not only the heart that pumps blood; it also applies to the whole inner self. This is the reason that King Solomon tells us in Proverbs 4:23 to guard our hearts. Turning negative thoughts into positive ones requires being mindful of the things we think about and give our attention to. If we want God to take away the sadness and the pull of despair that comes with it, we must be intentional about what we decide to replace those thoughts with. The apostle Paul gives us wise counsel about what to fix our thoughts on in Philippians 4:8, like the things that are good, true, and praiseworthy. Prior to that, in verses 6–7, he reminds us not to worry about anything, to pray about everything, and to be thankful. And when we do these things, he promises that "the peace of God, which surpasses all understanding, will guard your hearts and your minds in Christ Jesus." We can be assured that when we ask God to guard our hearts, He will honor our request. In his book *Renovation of the Heart: Putting on the Character of Christ*, Dallas Willard writes, "The most obvious thing we can do is to draw certain key portions of Scripture into our minds and make them a part of the permanent fixtures of our thought. This is the primary discipline for the thought life."

Reflect: How can you be careful with your thoughts?

Prayer: Lord, at times, I feel as if I am sinking in my negative thought pattern. Forgive me for letting negativity have power over how I feel. Fill me with optimism. Guard my heart and help me to learn to transform my thoughts. In Jesus's name, amen.

Thirty-Three

Good Thoughts

Finally, brothers, whatever is true, whatever is honorable, whatever is just, whatever is pure, whatever is lovely, whatever is commendable, if there is any excellence, if there is anything worthy of praise, think about these things.

Philippians 4:8

I have a scar about twelve inches long on my left thigh that resulted from the incision made during cancer surgery. The surgeons used the thigh's tissue and blood vessels to reconstruct the right side of my face, knowing that there would be a void in this area once the affected gland and surrounding lymph nodes were removed. It still amazes me how my thigh muscle became such a pivotal part of surgery involving the cancerous gland in my mouth. I started to pay a lot more attention to the thigh muscle, also known as the sartorius ("mender") muscle. It is the biggest and strongest muscle in our bodies, and it allows the lower body to flex, bend, and rotate. I recalled that two days after surgery, a nurse helped me sit up in bed.

It was a movement that required every ounce of energy. I placed my feet on the ground, got up, and slowly walked a short way down the hospital hallway using a walker, barely able to move either of my legs and unable to bend them.

Two weeks after surgery, I was able to move around with more agility. I was hopeful and excited about regaining my strength. I needed strong thighs and legs to enjoy my favorite sports: golf, tennis, hiking, and biking. I remember a client sharing these words with me weeks earlier: "Keep a positive mindset and remember the body is capable of healing itself." She was right. My body was healing on its own, and this gave me hope. Dr. Caroline Leaf, a cognitive neuroscientist, believes that "what we are thinking every moment of every day becomes a physical reality in your brain and body, which affects your mental and physical health." This means that a hopeful mindset requires being mindful of the things we think about and give our attention to. Paul emphasizes in the book of Philippians that we should direct our minds toward uplifting and virtuous thoughts: "Whatever is true, whatever is honorable, whatever is just, whatever is pure, whatever is lovely, whatever is commendable, if there is any excellence, if there is anything worthy of praise, think about these things." (Philippians 4:8). Such thoughts will keep us hopeful regardless of the health challenges, events, or circumstances in our lives.

Reflect: How can you direct your mind toward the more uplifting thoughts that Paul was speaking about in today's Bible verse?

Prayer: Lord, You are the great physician and healer. Help me to have uplifting and virtuous thoughts when dealing with various trials. In Jesus's name, amen.

Thirty-Four

Nothing Will Be Impossible

Ah, sovereign Lord, you have made the heavens and the earth with your great power and outstretched arm. Nothing is too hard for you.
Jeremiah 32:17, NIV

While on this rigorous cancer journey, I occupied my mind with engaging activities such as drawing, painting, playing word games, and building puzzles. Drawing allowed me to share my love of art with others through the pieces I produced. I also spent time cooking new recipes, socializing, laughing along with the silly videos I saw on social media, asking more questions and gaining understanding about my next steps, and always giving thanks in everything. Pushing myself to participate in these activities really allowed me to redirect my thoughts, time, and energy away from things that could not change my prognosis—about the possibility of a recurrence of this rare and aggressive type of salivary gland cancer. Doctors have told me that I will need CT/PET scans every three months for the next couple of years to detect the presence of cancer in my body. It is not a sure thing that I will ever be cancer-free. But this is not to say that this is impossible, medically, or otherwise. If God wills it, then I will be cancer-free because "nothing will be impossible" (Luke 1:37) and "What is impossible for people is possible with God," as Jesus taught his disciples in Luke 18:27 (NLT).

When the prophet Jeremiah was confined in prison and Jerusalem was being besieged, God's promise to restore the land seemed impossible. But Jeremiah prayed, "Ah, sovereign Lord, you have made the heavens and the earth with your great power and outstretched arm. Nothing is too hard for you" (Jeremiah 32:17). Did you catch that? Jeremiah was looking at the awesome power of God, which nothing could match. He was looking at the big picture. Today, we seem to get lost in the pressing needs that are set before us at the expense of losing sight of our God's infinite power over all things. This reminds me of some overwhelming challenges leading up to my cancer diagnosis, one of which was writing my first book on the connection between food and mental health. I thought it would be very difficult to complete this work within a year, given that there was a lot of research that had to be done. And besides, I was a nutritionist but by no means an expert in the mental health arena. Then, halfway through the writing process, I lost my inspiration to write because I was grieving my father's sudden passing. It was also during this same time that my terrible, mysterious jaw pain was becoming a major distraction. But I persisted when I remembered that the sovereign Lord, who is my strength, gives us grace to endure and to finish what I believe He started in the first place. The book was completed one month before my next daunting life event—a diagnosis of cancer.

No situation is impossible or hopeless with God. He can do anything for the accomplishment of His purposes. When God commands us to do what we think is difficult or impossible, He will empower us to carry it out through the work of the Holy Spirit within us.

Reflect: What difficult situation can you commit to God today?

Prayer: Lord, You are sovereign. Help me to surrender my impossibilities to You so that You may transform them into opportunities. In Jesus's name, amen.

Thirty-Five

Walk by Faith

For we walk by faith, not by sight.
2 Corinthians 5:7

Like many people dealing with an illness, my body, mind, and emotions cycled continuously through periods of joy, pain, discouragement, and discomfort. But the level of testing of my faith that accompanied it all has certainly reshaped me and who I have become. Looking back over the journey—from the removal surgery, reconstruction of my face, a radiation treatment, and physical therapy—I really had no idea how each minute, hour, or day would unfold. I knew I had a faith foundation, but like many people, I did not know what this foundation was able to withstand. To be certain, my faith has been strengthened through it all. Yet I still need strength to help me look past the obstacles like the need for follow-up visits, to see doctors and get CT/PET scans and mammograms every three months, six months, or yearly. I am slowly adapting to my new look and the constant numbness on the right side of my face and around my right ear and also around my neck. I will begin facial nerve rehabilitation therapy as soon as facial muscle movement begins on the paralyzed side of my face. This type of therapy will help me attain control over my facial muscles so that the movements feel more natural.

I do not know how successful facial therapy will be, just as I do not know about any of the results from future scans of my body. In facing all these and the multitude of other unknowns that are all around me, I am content that I must, more than ever, "walk by faith, not by sight," as the apostle Paul urges us in 2 Corinthians 5:7. Although Paul was not literally talking about the physical ability of walking and seeing, I thought about how blessed I am to have those abilities. Those who are blind often need a guide dog, cane, or another person holding their hand to guide them in the right direction. This is blind faith—a faith that is not self-reliant and one that is trusting completely in the dark without knowing how hard or easy the road is ahead. As He guides me to my destination, God is using my walk through the path of cancer, through the darkest valley of my life, for His glory. Yes, it is He who is leading and teaching me to walk every day in the Spirit so that I might be a beacon of light to a world that needs to see Him.

Walking by faith can be scary and difficult at times for all of us. But God has called us to trust Him with all our hearts (Proverbs 3:5) in every aspect of our lives. We need to ask Him to blindfold us and lead us by faith to the place where He wants us to go.

"Faith is taking the first step even when you don't see the whole staircase."
—Martin Luther King, Jr.

Reflect: What does your walk of faith look like?

Prayer: Thank You for teaching me to walk every day in the Spirit.

Please help me to walk by faith, to live by faith, and to trust all Your promises. Give me the strength I need to take the next step. In Jesus's name, amen.

Thirty-Six

Inner Beauty

It has been extremely hard to look at photos of myself smiling, that is, photos before cancer surgery changed that smile. When I look in the mirror or take a photo now, all I can see is the fold and drooping lip on the right side of my face. I no longer feel beautiful based on my outward appearance. Many people have told me that I "look wonderful," that they love me, and that I am beautiful on the inside and outside. I am grateful for their kind words, which inspire me to say the same things to myself.

I know deep down on the inside that it should not matter how we look on the outside, but the world puts so much focus on external beauty, and most, if not all, of us have bought into this idea. It is as if the outward appearance is more important than the inner character. In our society, women are often valued for their looks, and when their looks fade, it is sometimes frowned upon if she keeps her gray hair, for example. The Bible makes it clear to "not let your adorning be external—the braiding of hair and the putting on of gold jewelry, or the clothing you wear—but let your adorning be the hidden person of the heart with the imperishable beauty of a gentle and quiet spirit, which in God's sight is very precious" (1 Peter 3:3–4). This verse really resonated with me when a good friend and coworker wrote, "Whatever ways your physical appearance has changed, this will not affect my love and appreciation for the person you are or for our long relationship of mutual caring and respect."

We are also reminded about the Lord's perspective when it comes to outward appearance. He pointed this out to Samuel while searching for the next ruler of Israel—"The Lord does not look at the things people look at. People look at the outward appearance, but the Lord looks at the heart" (1 Samuel 16:7). We must be careful not to take on the world's perspective of beauty, which we all can agree has been embedded in most of us since we were children. God looks at our hearts and sees our motives and character. He knows everything there is to know about us (Psalm 139:1). Just as a flower bends toward the light to bloom and grow, so should we turn to the light of God to see the inner beauty that comes through God's sustaining and strengthening power.

Reflect: What steps can you take to reflect more on the inner beauty of those inside and outside of your circle?

Prayer: Lord, thank You that You know everything about me and that You can truly see my inner beauty and heart. Help me to look beyond outward appearances and to remember that my beauty comes from within. In Jesus's name, amen.

Thirty-Seven

Power of Prayer

Before becoming a believer, I thought prayer was reciting formal prayers such as the Lord's Prayer that Jesus taught His disciples (Matthew 6:9–13). But prayer is much more than recitation. According to Billy Graham, the renowned evangelist and preacher, "Prayer is spiritual communication between man and God, a two-way relationship in which man should not only talk to God but also listen to Him." And it is not about talking to yourself! The Bible mentions that "This is the confidence we have in approaching God: that if we ask anything according to his will, he hears us" (1 John 5:14, NIV). Furthermore, prayer is consistent and continuous communication with God. Jesus knew what God wanted because He was always in the habit of praying (Luke 5:16), and the apostle Paul encourages us to "pray without ceasing" (1 Thessalonians 5:16). Additionally,

Jesus teaches us to persistently ask, seek, and knock through prayer (Matthew 7:8).

Thirty years ago, I participated in an in-depth, structured, and interdenominational Bible study program known as Bible Study Fellowship (BSF). While studying the gospel of John at BSF, I became a believer in Jesus Christ and established a relationship with Him. Since that time, I have learned to value prayer as a means of communication with God. I learned how to pray using a four-step ordered outline: adoration, confession, thanksgiving, and supplication, or ACTS. While some may say that this approach is formulaic, I found that it helps me to focus on building my relationship with God and increase my understanding of who God is and what He wants me to do. Through the daily lessons and teachings from the Bible at BSF, I began my journey to create real deep spiritual roots. The Bible says, "Let your roots grow down into him, and let your lives be built on him" (Colossians 2:7, NLT). While on my cancer journey, prayer has become a sharper tool in my life. I have begun to pray with more specificity in the morning and at night, praising Him freely and spontaneously, and trusting that God's purposes are accomplished in my struggles.

Prayers do not have to be complex but should be sincere with the goal of building and strengthening your relationship with Jesus Christ. If you need help in this area of your journey, feel free to follow my lead with the prayers written in this devotional. In time, you will develop and use your own method for praying. The daily time spent communicating heart-to-heart with God and the prayers of many people can bring you peace and comfort during difficult times.

Reflect: How are you making prayer a part of your life?

Prayer: God, help me to realize the power I have in prayer. Help me unleash the power of prayer in my life. Show me how to grow closer to You in prayer. In Jesus's name, amen.

Thirty-Eight

Give Thanks

> *Give thanks in all circumstances; for this is the will of God in Christ Jesus for you.*
> 1 Thessalonians 5:18

One of the many get-well cards that I received was from a dear friend during my illness. It read, "Our God is the great physician—the one who mends you and knows how to heal you. His healing touch restores the body, mind, and spirit. His schedule is never too full. His diagnosis is always accurate. His treatment is wise and gentle. And his results are amazing!" This card described exactly how I pictured God. I received many other thoughtful greeting cards like this one, along with live plants, flowers, daily verses, and inspirational quotes, which provided emotional support and helped with the healing process. I am grateful for all these precious gifts as well as the love and encouragement I received from all my loved ones, friends, members of my church family, and Bible study groups who were right there with me throughout this journey.

In my daily journal, I recorded my gratitude for the many things God was showing me along the way. As I went back and read through each entry in the journal, I noticed that it was easier to give thanks on the days when I was doing well. When I was feeling overwhelmed, I was not very thankful because my ill health sometimes clouded my focus on how much our God provides. But thankfulness to God should be done every day, no matter how we are feeling or whether that day calls for thankfulness or not. Paul tells the believers at Thessalonica to give thanks *in* all circumstances (1 Thessalonians 5:18), not *for* all circumstances. King Jehoshaphat told the people of Judah, who were facing war, "Give thanks to the Lord, for his faithfulness is everlasting" (2 Chronicles 20:20).

We always have plenty of good reasons to express our thankfulness to God. The psalmist leads us with this example of adoration: "It is good to give thanks to the Lord, to sing praises to your name, O Most High" (Psalm 92:1). Being thankful reminds us that our focus should be on God and not on ourselves. Every moment of the day, I look for insights and ways to show my gratitude to God in all things. I practice gratitude by thinking of three instances of God's goodness or something I can be thankful for and write them down.

Reflect: What is one way you can implement an attitude of thanksgiving into your life?

Prayer: God, Your faithfulness is everlasting. Thank You for Your goodness and for being who You are. Help me to know that no matter what happens in my life, I always have something to be thankful for. In Jesus's name, amen.

Thirty-Nine

⤬

Big Mistake

But he said to me, "My grace is sufficient for you, for my power is made perfect in weakness." Therefore, I will boast all the more gladly of my weaknesses, so that the power of Christ may rest upon me.

2 Corinthians 12:9

In the months following surgery and rehabilitation, I was very thankful for all God had helped me to enjoy again. Still, there were some recurring thoughts that I seemed to have about the period of months leading up to the cancer diagnosis in the spring of 2023. I kept remembering the excruciating and continuous pain that I had experienced in my right jaw beginning around August 2022. Thinking that it could possibly be a toothache, I had gone to see my dentist, but she referred me to an endodontist who performed a root canal. This did not relieve the pain. Next was a referral to a dentist who specializes in jaw pain. She recommended wearing special night guards to prevent grinding my teeth while sleeping. Days became weeks, and weeks became months, but the pain was not going away. The first of two ENT doctors who I would ultimately see while on this journey could not find the cause, nor could he explain why there was swelling in the right parotid gland, indicated on a CT scan. So without much explanation, he referred me to a rheumatologist, thinking that my symptoms must be related to an autoimmune condition such as Sjogren's syndrome, lupus, or rheumatoid arthritis. None of these medical professionals had been able to zero in on an accurate root cause or a possible cure during all this time. It was not until I was miraculously referred to the second ENT doctor eight months after the onset of my jaw pain that a glimmer of hope came into focus.

Once I received the cancer diagnosis, I looked inward and started to question myself about what wrong turns, if any, I may have taken. The main recurring questions in my mind were why did I wait so long to find a different ENT physician who would have listened and taken my complaints seriously? Would that step have perhaps caught the cancer at an earlier stage? Would the tumor have been smaller and not spread to the surrounding lymph nodes? These questions in my mind plagued me for a very long time. I was beating myself up for not being more proactive about my own health. We often do this to ourselves when we feel like we have made big mistakes or messed up. We feel ashamed, like Peter must have felt when he denied knowing Jesus three times (Luke 22:54–62). But God is not making us feel bad about our mistakes—actual or perceived. We are reminded in 2 Corinthians 12:9 that God's grace (limitless blessings or unmerited favor we do not deserve) is sufficient for us. This includes when we feel weak and powerless about something in our past that is haunting us. I am convinced that He used this situation about any of my presumed mistakes to instead show me areas in my life that needed to change, like spending more time communicating with Him about each day and about my future.

Reflect: Is there a mistake you are holding on to that you need to release to God?

Prayer: God, You are gracious. Thank You for Your grace, which is sufficient for me. Please release me from my past mistakes that I may be holding on to and help me to reflect more on Your grace. In Jesus's name, amen.

Forty

Looking Forward

> *Be strong and courageous. Do not fear or be in dread of them, for it is the LORD your God who goes with you. He will not leave you or forsake you.*
>
> *Deuteronomy 31:6*

At the time of this writing, I have completed radiation treatments, and physical therapy. The vision in my right eye is excellent, although it is extremely dry and irritable sometimes. I have no hearing loss. I can turn my neck and shoulders enough to play golf and tennis. I can walk a few miles per day and ride a stationary bicycle most days of the week. And most of all, I can now look forward to enjoying food again. With the desire and willingness to get better and the constant encouragement from loved ones and friends, I keep going. I feel stronger, hopeful, and so incredibly grateful with each passing day.

Every journey has a starting point, the journey itself, and a destination. As we travel through life, we may encounter events such as abundant sunshine, strong winds, torrential rain, drifting snow, or sometimes raging fires. The journey may have all kinds of twists and turns, detours, confusing traffic circles, sudden stops, and even rough patches. Throughout this cancer journey, I have experienced many difficulties, most of which seemed unbearable, unmanageable, and unfair. Yes, there were times when I wanted to give up, times when I cried out to God, saying, "I can't take it anymore. I just can't take it anymore!" However, I stayed on the path by my faith, tethered to God's grace, and His promise that "When I pass through the waters, he will be with me; and through the rivers, they shall not overwhelm me; when I walk through fire, I shall not be burned, and the flame shall not consume me" (Isaiah 43:2).

The cancer journey is not over, and I have no idea what additional challenges lie ahead on my path. There will be unknown things that may sometimes sneak up and try to intimidate me about the future. Thus, I am determined to greet each day that I am blessed to behold with the things of which I am certain: that God is in control, His Word will sustain and strengthen me, His Spirit will revive me, His promises will never fail, and His plans will unfold as He proclaims. I look faithfully ahead and know that God will equip me with all I need to continue this journey.

I am moving forward not by faith in medical or other predictions but by faith in God's promises. By allowing the words of Deuteronomy 31:6 to echo over my life daily: "Be strong and courageous. Do not fear or be in dread of them, for it is the LORD your God who goes with you. He will not leave you or forsake you."

Reflect: What fears and concerns about the future can you give over to God today as you look into the future?

Prayer: Lord, help me to throw away my fear and to be strong and courageous. Remind me that You will walk with me and will not leave me as I move forward on my journey. In Jesus's name, amen.

Bibliography

Introduction
Sorge, Bob. *Secrets of the Secret Place. Legacy Edition.* Grandview, Mo: Oasis House, 2021.

April Fools' Day
"Parotid Tumors." Mayo Clinic. Last Modified April 26, 2023. https://www.mayoclinic.org/diseases-conditions/parotid-tumor/cdc-20388269.

Greater Things to Come
Weaver, Joanna. *Having a Mary Heart in a Martha World.* Colorado Springs, CO: Waterbook Press, 2000. Kindle.

Holding It Together
"Positron Emission Tomography (PET)." NIH Clinical Center. Last modified May 19, 2022. https://clinicalcenter.nih.gov/pet/about_pet.html.

Joys Comes in the Morning
Stanley, Charles. *The Charles f. Stanley Life Principles Bible: New American Standard Bible.* Nashville: Thomas Nelson, 2009.

Strawberry Jell-O
Guzik, David. "Exodus 16 – Manna for the Children of Israel." Enduring Word. Accessed January 4, 2024. https://enduringword.com/bible-commentary/exodus-16.

Speechless
Stanley, Charles. *How to Let God Solve your Problems: 12 Keys to a Divine Solution.* Nashville, TN: Thomas Nelson, 2008. Kindle.

The Doctor and the Nurse
"Compassion." Cambridge Dictionary. Accessed January 13, 2024. https://dictionary.cambridge.org/es/diccionario/ingles/compassion.

Time Alone
Jeremiah, David. *Overcomer*. Nashville, TN: Thomas Nelson, 2018.

Good Thoughts
Leaf, Caroline. *Switch on your brain: The key to peak happiness, thinking, and health*. Grand Rapids, MI: BakerBooks, 2015.

Guard Your Heart
Willard, Dallas. *Renovation of the Heart-Putting on the Character of Christ*. Colorado Springs, CO: NavPress, 2002. Kindle.

Nothing Will Be Impossible, A Season, Our Burden
Gooden, Kathleen. *Practical ways to better mental health: Food and lifestyle strategies*. Self-published, IngramSpark, 2023.